CHEMISTRY

KINGFISHER
LONDON & NEW YORK

KINGFISHER
LONDON & NEW YORK

Text and design copyright © Toucan Books Ltd. 2010
Based on an original concept by Toucan Books Ltd.
Illustrations copyright © Simon Basher 2010

Published in the United States by Kingfisher,
120 Broadway, New York, NY 10271
Kingfisher is an imprint of Macmillan Children's Books, London.
All rights reserved.

Consultant: Nick Chatterton

Designed and created by Basher
www.basherscience.com

Dedicated to Emma Marbrook

Distributed in the U.S. and Canada by Macmillan, 120 Broadway,
New York, NY 10271

EU representative: Macmillan Publishers Ireland Ltd, 1st Floor, The Liffey
Trust Centre, 117-126 Sheriff Street Upper, Dublin 1, D01 YC43.

Library of Congress Cataloging-in-Publication data has been applied for.

ISBN: 978-0-7534-6413-7

Kingfisher books are available for special promotions and premiums.
For details contact: Special Markets Department, Macmillan,
120 Broadway, New York, NY 10271.

For more information, please visit www.kingfisherbooks.com

Printed in China
20 19 18
18TR/0422/WKT/UNTD/128MA

Note to readers: the website addresses listed above are correct at
the time of going to print. However, due to the ever-changing nature
of the Internet, website addresses and content can change. Websites
can contain links that are unsuitable for children. The publisher cannot
be held responsible for changes in website addresses or content, or
for information obtained through a third party. We strongly advise that
Internet searches be supervised by an adult.

CONTENTS

Introduction
Chemistry/Antoine Lavoisier

Welcome to the wonderful, wild, and sometimes wacky world of chemistry. Full of alchemy and mystery, it's the oldest of all the sciences. Chemistry is the study of the stuff the world is made from—the physical and chemical properties of matter—and how it behaves in chemical reactions. This is the field that has given humankind a hundred thousand snazzy new materials, not to mention an understanding of the inner workings of life itself.

Chemists may think they have all the solutions, but Antoine Laurent Lavoisier (1743–1794) had more than most. He realized that air was made of several parts and that a very important part of it is released by plants and is also combined with hydrogen to make water. He called this part oxygen. Another one of Lavoisier's findings was simple but fundamental to chemical reaction: what goes in (the reactants) always weighs the same as what comes out (the products). Sadly, he wasn't appreciated in his day and was beheaded during the French Revolution. It was his unpopular day job as a taxman that did it for this father of modern chemistry.

Antoine Lavoisier

CHAPTER 1
Basic States

Kicking things off is a straightforward, no-nonsense gang who take a back-to-basics approach. These are the things that you can see, touch, feel, and hold— matter. There's the basic building block of matter itself, Element (he's the one that really "matters,") and the ways it combines in Compoud and Mixture. You'll find it in three forms: Solid, Liquid, and Gas—the so-called "states of matter." The more frisky Melting Point and Boiling Point control when and how matter melts or boils and changes its character.

Solid

Liquid

Gas

Melting Point

Boiling Point

Brownian Motion

Element

Compound

Mixture

The Periodic Table

Solid
Basic States

* This stubborn old goat is the lowest-energy state of matter
* Chunky hunk whose particles have a rigid internal structure
* Heating makes its particles vibrate and melt into a liquid

Trustworthy and dependable, I don't go for anything showy or high-energy. I'm built well and meant to keep my shape. With high melting points, I definitely don't flow. I'll sit motionless instead, which is handy if you want to make objects out of me or use me to contain playful, slippery Liquid.

With my atoms closely packed together, I resist squeezing and changing volume. My atoms often have a crystal structure—a regularly repeating pattern—but certain solids, such as glass, have an amorphous (random) internal structure. Raising my internal energy (by heating me, for example) will eventually turn me to liquid. Polymers are solids with long, flexible molecules, making them plastic. Proteins are biological solids found in all living matter.

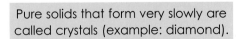

Pure solids that form very slowly are called crystals (example: diamond).

● Densest: osmium (23 x heavier than Water)
● Lightest: aerogel (530 x lighter than Water)
● Lightest metal: lithium (floats on Water)

Solid

Liquid

■ Basic States

※ This fluid fellow flows through your arteries and veins
※ A medium-energy state of matter that can't exist in a vacuum
※ Heating turns this guy into a gas; freezing turns him into a solid

Nothing much bothers me, man. Like an old-school beatnik, I'm easygoing and just go with the flow. If there are obstacles in my way, I work around them, and I change my shape easily to fit into any container you choose.

I'm an important fellow—without water on this planet, for example, life wouldn't be possible. But I am fussy about whom I mix with. Sometimes I slip right in with other liquids, but other times I flat out refuse. You can see this in the rainbow drops of oil in dirty puddles. Mutual attraction between my molecules causes surface tension, a force that makes me form drops. I resist being compressed, and I expand when heated. If you heat me up or decrease the pressure around me, I'll eventually evaporate away as gas. When I dissolve a solid, I'm called a solvent.

Liquid mercury, with its high surface tension, is actually dry!

● Number of liquid elements: 2
● Liquid elements: Bromine, Mercury
● Amount of bodyweight that's water: 70%

Liquid

Gas

■ Basic States

- ☀ This highest-energy state of matter has plenty of get-up-and-go
- ☀ A guy of no fixed shape or volume, with energy to burn
- ☀ Measured in °F or °C, and not greatly affected by pressure

I fizz, crackle, and pop—I literally hum with energy. Freed from the tiresome bonds that bind Solid and Liquid, my particles dart around like hyperactive bees.

I'm mischievous and can disappear right in front of your eyes, dispersing into thin air. Although I can be colored, like green chlorine gas, I am usually invisible, like the air all around you. My unconfined nature means that I have no choice but to fill any container that I am put into. Squeeze me into a can and my particles bash against the sides, exerting a force that is felt as pressure. Heating me up makes my particles move around faster and also has the effect of increasing the pressure. But squeeze me hard enough and you can calm down my exuberance enough to turn me into a Liquid. I can take the pressure; can you?

Mustard gas is very poisonous and was first used as a weapon in World War I.

- ● Lightest gas: hydrogen
- ● Heaviest gas 77 °F (25 °C): tungsten hexafluoride
- ● Heaviest element gas: radon

Gas

Melting Point
Basic States

* ✸ This sticky fellow is the point at which a solid turns liquid
* ✸ A measure of how easily forces inside solids are broken
* ✸ Measured in °F (or °C) but not affected by pressure

I'm soft and schmaltzy, and my crooning will melt Solid's heart. The forces between atoms and molecules in Solid are strong and stable, so it takes energy to break them. When you heat up a solid, its particles vibrate more and more until, finally, they have enough internal energy to break apart. Measure the temperature as Solid turns to mush, and you have found me!

Melting Point

When a solid turns directly into a gas, this is called sublimation.

* Melting point of ice (sea level): 32 °F (0 °C)
* Highest m.p. (element): 6683 °F (3695 °C)
* Lowest m.p. (element): –516 °F (–268.98 °C)

Boiling Point
Basic States

- ✸ The point at which a liquid boils and turns into a gas
- ✸ A measure of how easily forces inside liquids are overcome
- ✸ Measured in °F (or °C) and very obviously affected by pressure

Boiling Point

I'm a fiery cauldron fizzing with rage. Roiling and bubbling, I vent my fury on Liquid. The molecules that make up Liquid are much less tightly bound to each other than Solid's molecules are, but they still have a definite tendency to bunch together. I teach them to stand on their own two feet, by busting apart their intermolecular forces and turning them into a gas!

- ● Water boiling point (sea level): 212 °F (100 °C)
- ● Highest b.p. (element): 10040 °F (5560 °C)
- ● Lowest b.p. (element): –516 °F (–268.98 °C)

Water on top of Mount Everest boils at about 158 °F (70 °C).

15

Brownian Motion

Basic States

- Stinky browny-pants who shows how tiny particles move around
- Makes molecules bash blindly all over the place
- Thermal energy (heat) is the biggest mixer of molecules in liquids

For a chemistry thingamabob with such a sensible name, I am a very silly character. I say things like "nip skeep wibble wibble"—because everything about me is random! You might not be able to tell what I'm going to do next, but you can easily predict my overall random behavior.

I describe the way particles move around in liquid and gas. Seen under a microscope, a tiny pollen grain will jitter around in water as if it's alive—well, that's what Mr. Brown first thought. Mr. Einstein figured out that the "random walk" happens because the particle is being battered around by the invisible motion of molecules in the liquid. This explains how smells spread: by a process of diffusion, stinky molecules are jostled and dispersed until . . . Ew, who let that one go?

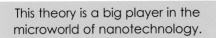

This theory is a big player in the microworld of nanotechnology.

- Named after Robert Brown (1827)
- First recorded by Jan Ingen-Housz (1785)
- First explained by Albert Einstein (1905)

Brownian Motion

Element
Basic States

- ☀ A kind of goody two-shoes that makes up every substance
- ☀ Elementary character made of atoms of all the same type
- ☀ One of the building blocks of matter, listed in the periodic table

Pure and simple, I am the basic stuff of everything that you see in the universe. With my 118 unique versions there's no limit to the possible combinations I can make, there's already a mind-boggling number of compounds in existence. Chemists continue to make new ones by combining me in different proportions or in new ways.

Each of my versions is a unique variety made up of just one type of Atom. My lightest variety is hydrogen, with a single proton in its nucleus. Next up is helium, with two protons and two neutrons. This pattern continues all the way to the strange, unstable, and very short-lived elements with a hundred or more protons (and attendant cargo of neutrons) in their central nuclei.

The most reactive metal is francium; the most reactive nonmetal is fluorine.

- No. of naturally occuring elements: 92
- Most common: hydrogen
- Heaviest: element 118 (ununoctium)

Element

Compound

■ Basic States

✳ This chemical master chef combines elements into new substances
✳ Produced and broken apart by Chemical Reaction
✳ Most substances on Earth exist in the form of compounds

My creations are the perfect pudding—a combination of all the right elements in just the right proportions. Chemicals like to cozy up with each other, and with the help of ionic and covalent bonding, I allow them to do this in a way that benefits both elements. But once my ingredients have been fused together, it's difficult to separate them.

Compound

Oxygen is a compound of two oxygen atoms (O_2).

● Total no. of known compounds: 61 million
● Ionic compound example: salt
● Covalent compound example: Water

Mixture

Basic States

* This mixed-up puppy is one smooth blender
* His recipes can be separated by physical means
* Chemical Reaction takes no part in this kind of combination

Mixture

I'm a real smoothie. I blend substances together—there's no sweat, none of Compound's heated reactions, just a relaxed merging of one substance with another. Like a sack of Halloween candy, I'm all mixed up, but each part can still be separated by physical means (such as with your sticky fingers!). Liquid mixtures need to be separated using special techniques, like distillation.

● Solid mixture examples: concrete, soil
● Liquid mixture (solution) ex.: salt water
● Solid-liquid mixture example: milk

Tap water is a mixture; distilled water is a pure substance.

The Periodic Table
Basic States

* An elegant way of organizing all known elements into a table
* Groups run vertically, and periods run horizontally
* Invented by the Siberian superchemist Dmitri Mendeleev in 1869

Hup-two! Hup-two! I'm a parade-ground sergeant major, and it's my job to get the elements in order. I whip these chemicals into shape. Yessirree!

A stickler for organization, I get all 118 elements to line up in groups, rows, and blocks. Groups (vertical columns) of elements share similar properties. Periods (horizontal rows) each represent a new energy level filled up with electrons. The type of substance and its chemistry (reactivity) changes as you move down a group or move along a period, depending on whether an element is happier to lose or gain electrons from its outer shell. In fact, you can tell an element's personality based on where it is in the table. Metals cluster on the left-hand side and nonmetals on the right.

Element 101, Mendelevium, is named after Mendeleev.

* Group 1: reactive metals
* Elements in center: transition metals
* Group 18: inert, or noble, gases

The Periodic Table

CHAPTER 2
Nuts and Bolts

Modest and unassuming, this bunch of founding fathers is rarely glimpsed. Yet these backroom movers and shakers are the are the prts that make up matter—the stuff from which the whole universe is made! Their properties govern the stately flow of energy as bonds uncouple and relink, as atoms and molecules move from one compound to another. And it's their behind-the-scenes activities that underpin chemical reactions and give the Lab Rats all the bubble and explosion they need. You have to keep your "Ion" this bunch; they're nuts!

Atom

Isotopes

Ion

Simple Molecule

Giant
Molecule

Polymer

Metallic
Bonding

Nanoparticles

Avogadro's
Number

Mole

Smart Materials

Atom
■ Nuts and Bolts

✴ Smaller than a pinprick but larger than life
✴ Atomic particle that has no overall electrical charge
✴ The Periodic Table is arranged in atomic number order

I am the stuff the universe is made of. I'm every chemical compound—in fact, I'm everything that you can see, touch, and breathe. I am like a planetary system in miniature. My central nucleus is made up of tightly packed, positively charged protons and neutral neutrons. Orbiting in energy levels (called shells) around this heavy, positive core are my zippy, negatively charged electrons. The shells wrap around the nucleus like the layers of an onion and are filled from the bottom up. The first shell holds two electrons, the second holds eight, and the third holds 18.

I hold on to my protons and neutrons for dear life. The number of protons determines what type of element I am, but it's the electrons in my outer shell that I use for chemistry, by pairing-and-sharing with other atoms or by moving them across to other atoms to create ions.

Half a million atoms could line up across a single human hair.

● No. of electrons = no. of protons
● Atomic number = no. of protons
● Mass number = no. of protons + neutrons

Atom

Isotopes
■ Nuts and Bolts

- ✸ Atoms with equal atomic numbers but different mass numbers
- ✸ Goblins with varying numbers of neutrons in their atomic nucleus
- ✸ Isotopes that decay (break apart) are called radioisotopes

Like the ghastly creations of some crazed scientist in a low-budget sci-fi movie, we're Atom's monstrous brothers. With the same number of protons as our atomic sibling, we have the same chemistry and undergo the same reactions. However, we have a different number of neutrons in our nuclei—sometimes more, sometimes less.

This unhealthy number of neutrons gives us a nasty streak. A normal atom is usually stable, but our unbalanced cores can lose protons and neutrons, or gain protons, in nuclear radiation, changing element type in the process! Medicine makes good use of our radioactive decay, but we are most famous for our destructive power: radon isotopes in granite give people cancer, while uranium-235 and plutonium-239 are the active ingredient in nuclear weapons.

Doctors use barium isotopes to trace the passage of food through the guts.

- ● Carbon 12 (6 protons, 6 neutrons) = ^{12}C
- ● Carbon 14 (6 protons, 8 neutrons) = ^{14}C
- ● Carbon 14: used in carbon dating

Isotopes

Ion

■ Nuts and Bolts

☀ An atom that has gained or lost one or more electrons
☀ Strong electrostatic forces hold these guys together
☀ Makes metals and nonmetals connect in "salty" crystal lattices

Let's get this party started! It's all well and good to admire Atom's steadiness, but you want a bit of spark and pizzazz in your chemistry set, don't you?

No atom, apart from the Group 8 elements, has a full set of electrons in its outer shell. My trick is to transfer electrons to or from the outer shells to fill them up. This creates positively and negatively charged ions, making lots of exciting chemical reactions possible—opposites attract! I join positive metal and negative nonmetal ions together in a tight embrace with my ionic bonds. The "ionic compounds" are rock-solid with high melting and boiling points; brittle crystals that dissolve in polar solvents (like water); and conductors of electricity when molten or in solution.

Table salt (sodium chloride) is a well-known ionic compound.

● Groups 1 & 2 (metals): lose electrons
● Groups 6 & 7 (nonmetals): gain electrons
● Melting point of salt NaCl: 1474 °F (801 °C)

Ion

Simple Molecule
■ Nuts and Bolts

* Two or more atoms held together by a covalent bond
* Covalent bonding shares electrons between atoms
* This calm character often forms between non-metals

There's nothing flashy about me. I am a safe pair of hands who is more like a geography teacher in a faded old suit than a superhero. Quiet and unfussy, I let two or more nonmetals combine, making electrically neutral, stable substances, such as Water and Nitrogen.

Rather than rob atoms of their electrons, transferring them around willy-nilly (like that shameless Ion), I prefer to allow nonmetal atoms to cooperate in filling their outer electron shells. This flexible and strong form of chemical bonding is called covalent bonding and is used by many simple molecules. My covalent compounds have low melting and boiling points because, although the bonds between atoms are strong, the forces of attraction between electrically neutral molecules are weak.

H_2O is a covalent compound of two hydrogen atoms and one oxygen atom.

● Bonds between atoms: very strong
● Intermolecular forces: very weak
● Smallest molecule: hydrogen (0.00000015mm)

Simple Molecule

Giant Molecule

Nuts and Bolts

* This diamond powerhouse is a girl's best friend
* Massive latticework with a huge number of bonds
* A titan who works best with carbon, silicon, and oxygen

I'm a covalent colossus, a behemoth of bonding. Atoms in my mammoth molecules are linked together by strong covalent bonds, like a towering superstructure of interlinked supports. Because each atom is tightly bonded to its neighbors, I am usually very hard, sometimes brittle, and have a very high melting point—and that's why diamonds are forever!

Giant Molecule

Carbon forms diamond, graphite, and insane spheres called buckyballs!

* Hardest mineral: diamond
* Melting/boiling point: very high
* Melting point of diamond: 6,500 °F (3,600 °C)

Polymer

Nuts and Bolts ■

※ Chains of small molecules form this "Mr. Poly" giant molecule
※ This multipurpose fellow comes in a thousand useful forms
※ Man-made plastics are the wonder material of the last century

Polymer

I'm plastic, and I'm possible because millions of simple, repeating hydrocarbon molecules (monomers) can connect to make giant, chainlink molecules. I have my naturally occurring varieties, but my man-made types, which are cheap to produce, can be anything you want them to be: pliable or rigid, soft or hard. For a groovy 1970s vibe, just check out polyester— it's like one long daisy chain!

● Natural polymers: cellulose, amber
● Man-made polymers: nylon, PVC
● Reaction called: polymerization

Used to make plastic bags, bottles, rubber boots, surgical implants . . .

Metallic Bonding

Nuts and Bolts

* Behind-the-scenes character that binds Metal's atoms together
* A lattice of positive ions surrounded by a sea of free electrons
* A big softie who is the reason why Metal is a good conductor

Inside the dark heart of that hard-case metalhead, Metal, you'll find me. One of three important types of chemical bonding, I link together metal atoms, just like ionic bonding links ions and covalent bonding chemically joins molecules.

The properties of metals are all down to the way I bind their atoms. Internally, metals are arranged into networks of positive ions with "seas" of electrons washing around in between them. Electrostatic forces of attraction between the ions and electrons hold the whole thing together, but the electrons are also free to move around through the giant structure. Because of this, metals are great conductors of heat and electricity. The flexible internal arrangement also allows metals to be shaped easily and hold to an edge well. I'm one sharp cookie!

Metals are shiny because light hits the sea of electrons and is reflected.

● Best conductor: Silver (1.59×10^{-8} Ωm)
● Hardest metal: tungsten carbide (8.9–9.5 Mohs)
● Melting point mercury: −101.90 °F (−38.83 °C)

Metallic Bonding

Nanoparticles
■ Nuts and Bolts

☀ No blockheads, these tiny particles have unusual properties
☀ Nanoparticles behave very differently to larger lumps of stuff
☀ They get added to materials to lend them superpowers

We live in the realm of the itty-bitty. Forget the flea: things in our world are just a few atoms wide. We are an array of dazzling shapes—cuboids, rods, spheres, and bananas—that are all 10,000 times thinner than a cat's whisker.

With each of our minuscule particles come unexpected talents. Let's take a lump of regular silver. It has the natural properties to kill bacteria and fungi, whereas a sprinkling of nanosilver acts as a ruthless killer of germs and superbugs. Why? Because it has much more surface area to its volume, which makes the atoms at its surface much more reactive and powerful. Sometimes it is just our teensy size that makes us special: zinc oxide nanos—amazing absorbers of UV light—are added to sunscreen because they're invisible to the naked eye.

Nanoparticles might have side effects on people and the environment.

● 1 nanometer = 0.000,000,001 meter
● Size of nanoparticle: 1–10 nm
● Nanoscience is called nanotechnology

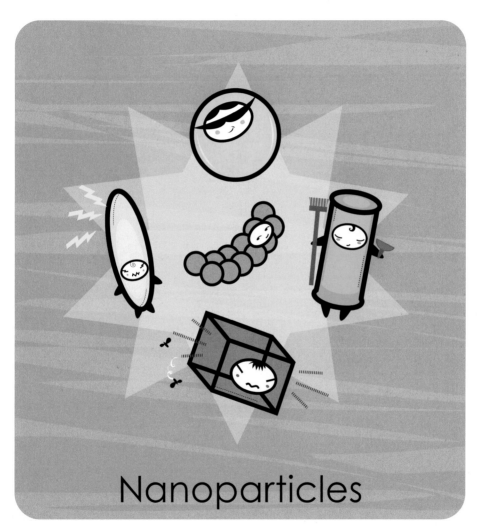

Nanoparticles

Avogadro's Number

Nuts and Bolts

✴ A real bigwig whose real name is the Avogadro constant
✴ A number that tells you how many molecules in a mole of Gas

You can count on me: I'm a constant. My special number—like a dozen eggs—tells you exactly how many atoms you will find in a specific quantity of any gas at a certain pressure and temperature. This number is 6022 followed by 20 zeros. It's a very big number; if you had that many cans of soda, they would cover the planet in a blanket 200 mi. (322km) thick!

Avogadro's Number

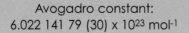

Avogadro constant:
$6.022\ 141\ 79\ (30) \times 10^{23}\ mol^{-1}$

● Named after: Amedio Avogadro
● 602,200,000,000,000,000,000,000 = no. of particles in one mole of substance

Nuts and Bolts ■

* This refined fellow isn't a mole who lives in a hole!
* A unit of measurement—or high-minded chemical counting!
* One mole (symbol: mol) has 6.02×10^{23} particles

Mole

Atoms are very small and devilishly difficult to count, so I help out with a useful piece of backward thinking. A one-mole serving of any element or compound always contains the same number of atoms or molecules, as given by Avogadro's Number. The weight of each mole is equal to the atomic mass of each element, measured in grams (for example, 1 mole of elemental oxygen = 16g).

● Mass of 1 mole of substance = molar mass
● 1 mole = the number of particles in 12g of pure carbon

One mole of gaseous oxygen (O_2) =
$16 \times 2 = 32g$

Smart Materials

■ Nuts And Bolts

☀ Futuristic new materials with amazing properties
☀ Sensitive souls who respond to heat, electricity, pH, and stress
☀ Sharp and intelligent . . . and out to change the world!

We're smart cookies! We point to a wild time ahead when materials will respond to changes in the external environment. But don't think we're only sci-fi make-believe. One member of our gang includes the super voltage-sensitive (electrochromic) material in LCDs that changes the color and transparency of an LCD screen.

We can give metals and plastics a "memory" by sprinkling in some nanoparticles. Our technology is also used in some glasses frames: squash them and our shape-memory alloy (SMA) will bend back to its original shape, without any help from you! We can even "learn" certain behavior. One day your toilet seat will warm up when you sit on it, your wallpaper will play music when you enter a room, and your fridge will change color to suit your mood. Sweet!

Cornstarch with water is an SM—its gloopiness alters when it's smacked!

● First used: early 1980s
● Smart memory plastics called: SMPs
● Common SMA: nitinol (nickel-titanium alloy)

42

Smart Materials

CHAPTER 3
Nasty Boys

Quick! On with the safety goggles and gloves—the bad boys of chemistry are on the loose! This caustic crew are the original chemical nasties, causing chaos wherever (and on whomever) they land. Belligerent bullies they may be, but the ability of Acid and Base to take to Water and release reactive ions gets them involved in lots of reactions. Sure, they push their weight around, but don't underestimate their usefulness to chemists and industry. They have their judges, too: pH is measured with Universal Indicator, which tells you how strong each bad boy is.

Acid

Base

pH

Universal Indicator

Acid
■ Nasty Boys

☀ A searing chemical nasty with a low pH
☀ Donor of positive H^+ ions, it's the chemical opposite of Base
☀ Wear gloves when handling this sour old soul

The most notorious of the Nasty Boys, I'm mad, bad, and thoroughly dangerous to know. Given the chance, I'll eat through metals and burn your skin!

What gives me my acidic nature is my ability to lose hydrogen ions. I'm a sinister splitter: in the presence of Water, I disassociate, breaking into a negative ion and a positive hydrogen ion (H^+). This little plus-fella is a spare proton (which is why I'm also called a proton donor). It's free to react with other chemicals in a solution and can then create ten kinds of havoc! Really strong acids instantly let loose 100 percent of their H^+ ions, while weak acids disassociate much less. Strong sulfuric acid is number one in the chemicals industry; weak acetic acid is number one when sprinkled on your salad as vinegar.

Phosphoric acid eats rust and makes carbonated drinks taste good!

● Strong but mild: carborane superacid
● Weak but corrosive: hydrogen fluoride
● Acid pH: numbers less than 7

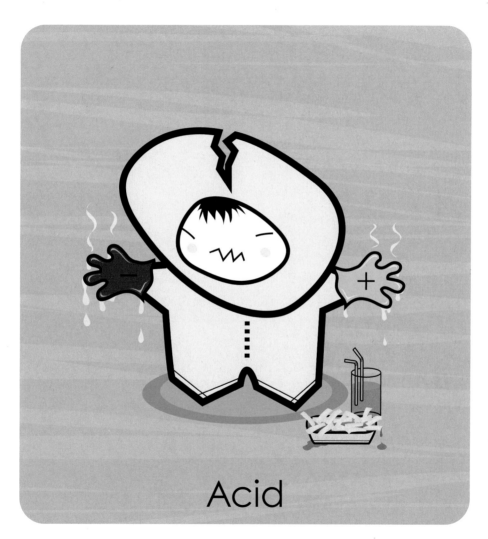

Acid

Base

Nasty Boys

- A basic chemical bad guy with a high pH
- Donor of negative OH^- ions, it's the chemical opposite of Acid
- Wear gloves when handling this caustic crony

I'm a lowdown, cheatin' gunslinger. Base by nature, Base by name—"Base" is the chemical way of saying that solutions containing me have a pH above 7. My most common types are called alkalis. These are hydroxides of alkali metals or alkaline earth metals (Groups 1 and 2 of the periodic table) that give basic solutions in Water. All alkalis are bases, but not all bases are alkalis. Ammonia —found in bleach—is a base but not an alkali.

Acids play fast and loose with their positive H^+ ions, but I hoard them. I love them so much that when mixed with Water, I steal them from the H_2O molecules! This floods a solution with super-reactive OH^- ions (Water minus a hydrogen ion). Household cleaners with me on board wipe the floor . . . and then lick the toilet bowl clean!

Sodium hydroxide has the frightening ability to melt fat and unblock drains!

- Strong base: sodium hydroxide
- Weak base: ammonia
- Basic pH: numbers more than 7

Base

pH

■ Nasty Boys

✳ Measure of a solution's acidity or the amount of H^+ ions
✳ Relative scale: low values are acidic and high values are basic
✳ This "pHella" is crucial to body and ocean chemistry

I'm the "pHantom": a secret agent with the code name pH. That's right, you got it. Small p. Big H. I infiltrate solutions to probe them for acidic activity. I then assign a number, from 0 to 14, to every solution. The more H^+ ions drifting around, the more acidic they are and the lower the number. Calm and unbiased, pH 7 is my magic number who sits in the neutral zone. Above this, solutions are completely basic!

"pHenomenally" important in your body's tricky chemical environment, my pH has to be just right for a staggering number of complex reactions to go off "pHlawlessly." When you exercise, your blood gets ever so slightly more acidic, from CO_2 released by cells breaking down carbohydrates and fat for energy—but too much acid in your blood causes a total shutdown of your body systems!

The abbreviation pH stands for the "power of hydrogen."

● Blood pH: 7.4 (called "physiological pH")
● pH of pure, distilled water: 7
● pH of rainwater: about 5.2

pH

Universal Indicator

Nasty Boys

* Simple way of testing for pH
* Indicates pH values with a spectrum of colors
* This universal policeman is found on handy strips of paper

I'm the detective of the Nasty Boys. With such a dangerous group, it's nice to know that you have a friendly copper like me padding around nearby. When faced with an unknown solution, I let you know how acidic or basic it is. I inform you of what you're up against with a simple change of color.

I indicate the entire range of the pH scale: the values from 0 to 14. Actually, I am a cunning mixture of different substances that each change color at different values. I'm found in books of little tear-off strips, which can be dipped into mystery solutions to tell you their acidity. I'm also found in liquid form. My individual components can be used in chemistry tests, called titrations, which tell you the precise end point of a chemical reaction with a "blush" of color. This is one way to find the concentration and purity of a solution.

The pigment in red cabbage juice is a natural universal indicator.

● Red: indicates strong acid
● Green: indicates neutral
● Purple: indicates strong base

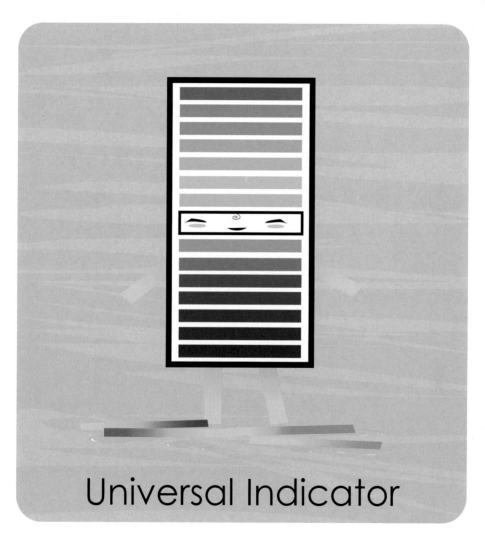

Universal Indicator

CHAPTER 4
Lab Rats

Bubble, bubble, toil, and trouble! This troop of madcap mavericks provide a playing field for some of science's most dangerous experiments. Their crazy shapes and twisted spirals of glass are a real "smash" and the material of choice for anyone intent on chemical capers, from the early alchemists who tried to turn lead into gold to the modern-day biochemist separating DNA on a gel and the inorganic chemist refluxing a super-duper new catalyst. Master the use of this equipment and you'll go a long way in chemistry—just remember, never lick the spoon!

Bunsen Burner

Thermometer

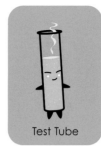

Test Tube

Pipette

Filter

Distillation

Precipitate

Chromatography

Bunsen Burner
■ Lab Rats

✴ Life's a natural gas for this burner who does hot work in the lab
✴ A "hole"-hearted fellow who heats, sterilizes, and combusts
✴ Burns between 1,380 °F (750 °C) and 1,740 °F (950 °C)

The undisputed king of the Lab Rats, I burn like a beacon, taking center stage in a theater of bangs, bubblings, and strange smells. I'm used for flame tests (to identify what type of metal is in a compound) and for heating stuff up.

The smart part of Mr. Bunsen's invention is an air hole at my base, near the gas inlet. With the hole fully open, the air-gas mixture is at its richest, allowing complete combustion and a roaring-hot flame. But watch out! On this setting, the flame burns a nearly invisible blue, with two very distinct cones—the hottest part is the inner cone. When you just need me on standby, switch to my cool, orange-yellow safety flame. Closing the hole allows the gas to mix with air only at the head of my chimney, which results in incomplete combustion and a safer, cooler flame!

Soot in the safety flame reflects light and makes it burn luminous yellow.

● Invented by Robert Bunsen (1854)
● Built by Peter Desdega (lab assistant)
● Fuel: natural gas (methane)

Bunsen Burner

Thermometer
■ Lab Rats

☀ A hothead who measures temperature in °F and °C
☀ Uses mercury or alcohol, which rises up the stem
☀ The stem is a very thin hollow tube of glass

I'm a little piece of magic that you can hold in your hand—a true chemical wizard. Heat is a very strange concept to pin down. It's something you can only feel. Until a liquid boils, for example, it's very difficult to see how hot or cold it is. Yet I turn that reality on its head and allow you to "see" temperature and read it off a calibrated (fixed) scale.

You have to handle me with care. I'm a delicate soul in a slender package. Surrounded by glass, my central column is a vacuum, which makes my liquid independent of air pressure. I work on the basis that materials expand and contract as they get hotter and colder. The longer my line, the higher the temperature reading. I am calibrated against known temperatures, such as the freezing and boiling points of water, to make sure I'm accurate.

From the Greek words for "heat" (*therme*) and "measure" (*metron*).

● Fahrenheit scale invented by G. Fahrenheit (1724)
● Celsius scale invented by A. Celsius (1742)

Thermometer

Test Tube

■ Lab Rats

✳ A chemical darling used to mix and store substances
✳ Made of special glass that doesn't expand when heated
✳ Sometimes has a stopper, or bung, to seal it up

Hold me, shake me, mix me, and heat me up! I'm the pinup of the lab. Made of glass, I'm slim, tall, and curved of lip, with a round bottom. I'm the playground on which most of chemistry—organic and inorganic—is played out. Finger-size, I usually lounge around in test-tube racks or am held tightly in the grip of a test-tube holder. Oh, I do love to cause a reaction!

Test Tube

An oxide of boron makes test-tube glass heat resistant.

● Made of Pyrex glass
● Length: 2 in. to 8 in. (50mm to 200mm)
● Width: 0.4 in. to 0.8 in. (10mm to 20mm)

* ☀ A cheeky little squirt used to transfer specific amounts of Liquid
* ☀ This chemical dropper is made of glass and rubber
* ☀ Delivers a smashingly accurate volume

Pipette

I'm a chemist's best friend. My simplest form looks like an eyedropper with a squeezable rubber bulb. You will find lots of different types of me in the lab, but my basic job is always the same: I suck up liquid from one container and deliver it to another as small squirts or drops. My fanciest model is the piston-driven micropipette, which delivers tiny amounts with great accuracy.

* ● Smallest: zeptoliter pipette
* ● Used with a burette for titration
* ● Micropipette invented by W. Gilson (1972)

Biochemists and forensic scientists use micropipettes.

Filter

■ Lab Rats

- ❋ A one-way door that allows only liquids or gases through
- ❋ Separates out solids that have gotten mixed with liquids or gases
- ❋ Firefighters rely on filters to breathe in smoke-filled buildings

I'm a canny operator who can get you out of a fix. Got Solid mixed up with Liquid? I make quick work of separating them. With the aid of a filter funnel and a cone of filter paper, I create a barrier that lets Liquid through but blocks Solid. No job is too small. You'll even find me making your coffee—well, filtering out the coffee grounds before you drink it.

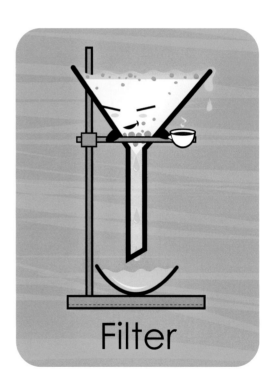

Filter

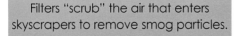
Filters "scrub" the air that enters skyscrapers to remove smog particles.

- ● Liquid that is filtered is called filtrate
- ● Solid left on paper is called residue
- ● Other uses: tea bags, fuel filters

Lab Rats ■

- ✳ This "moonshiner" is a method of separating and purifying liquids
- ✳ Rascally bubbler and boiler who separates crude oil into fractions
- ✳ Essential operator for the oil, plastics, and chemicals industries

Distillation

I'm a bootlegger and old-school scoundrel. My technique purifies and separates two or more liquids. Every liquid has a slightly different boiling point, so heating up a mixture of liquids brings each one to boil at a different temperature. In this way, I drive off the substance with the lowest boiling point first and collect it in a separate vessel.

- ● Earliest known use: 500 B.C.E.
- ● Fractional distillation separates crude oil into bitumen, diesel, jet fuel, petroleum

Used to make alcoholic drinks, such as whiskey, purer and more potent.

Precipitate
■ Lab Rats

✳ Standoffish solid formed in a solution during a chemical reaction
✳ Lets impurities be removed, or solids be produced, from solutions
✳ Used for making paint pigments and for making water safe to drink

Hanging like a gloomy cloud in a chemical mixture, I occur when an insoluble compound forms in a liquid mixture. Because of my unfriendly talents and refusal to mix in and make do, I am used to separate things out of liquids. Solids that don't dissolve in liquids are very handy because they will fall to the bottom of the liquid under gravity and settle on their own. Or they can be filtered out or even spun out of the solution in a centrifuge—now, that's a dizzying option!

I'm often mucky and nondescript, but sometimes I appear in the garish hues that any glowing neon sign would die for! In this guise, I am used in paint pigments. Potassium iodide added to lead nitrate, for example, results in a beautiful precipitate of bright yellow lead iodide. Yeowch!

Precipitation is used to remove the impurities from drinking water.

● Process called: precipitation
● Solid formed called: precipitate
● Liquid remaining called: supernate

Precipitate

Chromatography
■ Lab Rats

☀ Colorful crime investigator used by forensic scientists
☀ Separates the contents of complex mixtures for analysis
☀ Parts of a mixture travel at different speeds, which separates them

Anyone in need of a little TLC? Slide over here—I'm your main squeeze! Although chemists might need some Tender Loving Care every now and then, they're more likely to be happier with Thin-Layer Chromatography—ha ha! Joking aside, I'm a fully paid up Lab Rat. My analytical skills are used to make DNA fingerprints and this exciting crime-stopping streak brings some color to the lab!

I'm used to separate mixtures in a solution. Try me out for yourself. Just make a dot with a marker pen close to the bottom of a strip of filter paper, dip the end into a shallow dish of Water, and leave it overnight. As the water seeps up the paper column, the components in the ink mixture separate themselves out at different rates. This is exactly how CSI scientists analyze dye found at a crime scene.

From the Greek words for "color" (*chroma*) and "writing" (*graph*).

● Sample for analysis called: extract
● Types: paper, gas, liquid, "tlc"
● World's smallest column: 0.03 in. (1mm) 2010

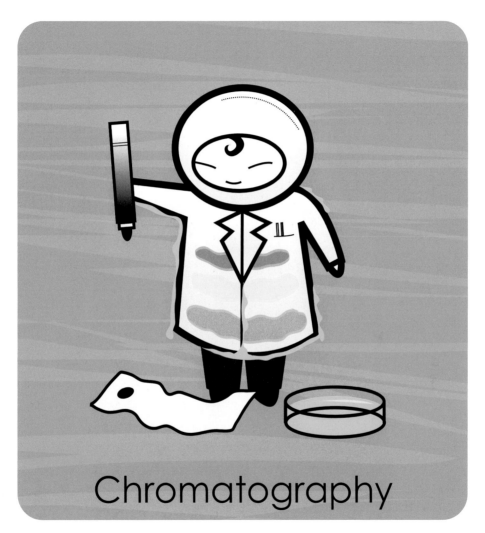

Chromatography

CHAPTER 5
Obnoxious Organics

Once upon a time, this group of compounds were thought to be made only by living organisms, so they were given the name "organic." But then some busybody chemist managed to make the sticky yellow substance urea (which occurs naturally in urine) in a lab using potassium cyanate and ammonium sulfate salts. Hmmm, nothing "organic" there. But the name was a good one, so it stuck. It now means the study of compounds of carbon—the basis of life on Earth. Hydrocarbons form the backbone of this chemical clan and of most organic compounds.

Hydrocarbons

Alcohol

Carboxylic Acids

Esters

Dyes

Hydrocarbons
■ Obnoxious Organics

* Slick molecules with skeletons made of hydrogen and carbon
* Almost all smarmy Hydrocarbons are derived from crude oil
* They are "cracked" (split) to produce new and useful chemicals

Howdy doody! We're the quick, slick oilman—a big-bucks Texas sugar daddy! Our smorgasbord of combustible compounds, produced by fractional distillation of crude oil, supplies much of the world's fuel. Don't think we're only good for fuel, though. We're cracked to produce a bunch of valuable chemicals, whom you're about to meet!

Our simplest version, called methane, has only one carbon atom with four covalently bonded hydrogen atoms—you release it when you fart. Simple Hydrocarbons like this are gases, but the melting and boiling points increase as the number of carbons in the chain increases. With five or six carbon atoms, we are liquids at room temperature; with increasing numbers, you'll find us as waxes, low-melting solids, and solid polymers.

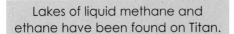
Lakes of liquid methane and ethane have been found on Titan.

● Formula of methane: CH_4
● First oil well drilled: Baku, Azerbaijan (1948)
● Largest oil reserves: Middle East (63% of total)

Hydrocarbons

Alcohol
Obnoxious Organics

- Liquid party animal who makes things go pop
- There are thousands of alcohols, including ethanol
- Ethanol is the colorless and volatile liquid in alcoholic drinks

I am very appealing, and many folk find me intoxicating company. But be careful, because I can bite hard. As ethanol—the active ingredient in alcoholic drinks—I am the world's most notorious depressant. Scratch my glitzy surface and you will find a drab, sad existence.

As a group of chemicals, however, I'm so much more than just ethanol. Glycol stays gloopy at very low temperatures, which makes it a handy antifreeze. My molecules are nothing more complicated than a hydrocarbon with an attached OH^- group. My OH^- group makes me "polar," with one slightly negatively charged and one slightly positively charged end. I'm also a super solvent for dissolving other polar compounds.

Yeast ferments sugar in ripe fruit to produce alcohol.

- Chemical formula ends in OH
- Formula of ethanol: C_2H_5OH
- Freezing point of ethanol: $-173°F$ $(-114°C)$

Alcohol

Carboxylic Acids
Obnoxious Organics

* Mostly natural, weak acids that are soluble in water
* Smelly compounds that can be made from alcohols or esters
* Reacts with alcohols to make esters

You can spot most of us a mile away, 'cause our names all end in "-oic." Methanoic acid (also called formic acid), for example, is a methane-based Carboxylic Acid. But we won't ruin your day—on the contrary, we're mild-mannered chemicals.

The Carboxylic Acids gang are brown-patches-on-the-elbows organic foodies, found in many natural products, such as coconut oil (lauric acid), milk (lactic acid), and vinegar (acetic acid). As salicylic acid, we provide pain relief in the form of aspirin, as well as treatments for warts and verrucas. We become more solid and waxy the longer our chains of carbon get—Carboxylic Acids with more than about ten atoms of carbon are called fatty acids, many of which are essential in the body.

Formic acid is the active ingredient in ant bites—and it stings!

● Chemical formula ends in COOH
● Formula of methanoic acid: HCOOH
● Odor: strong (think acetic acid in vinegar)

Carboxylic Acids

Esters

Obnoxious Organics

- Fragrant food flavorings that are insoluble in water
- Found in perfumes, body hormones, plus fruits and berries
- Made from carboxylic acid and alcohol; smell of nail polish

We're one fruity fancy! Wreathed in the fragrant fug of a flowery bouquet, our molecules can be all the flavors and colors of a scented eraser collection: strawberry, cherry, lavender . . . you name it. When fresh, we give taste and smell to many natural fruits and berries; when fake, we're the main ingredient for artificial food flavorings. Just suck on a lemon drop. That acidic "fruit flavor" is probably us!

We're made in the pretty-sounding esterification reaction, when a carboxylic acid reacts with an alcohol. (To make the peary smell in pear candy, for example, pentanol is added to ethanoic acid.) You can whiff us in the air because we're more volatile than Carboxylic Acids and prone to evaporation. At full strength, we're found in industrial solvents. But we're more than just a fake flavor!

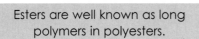

Esters are well known as long polymers in polyesters.

- Chemical formula ends in COOR
- Most sweet: ethylethanoate (pear drops)
- Most delicate: essential oils from plants

Esters

Dyes
Obnoxious Organics

* This fashionista's origins are lost in the mists of time
* Early dyes were made from plants and rusty earth pigments
* Embeds itself deep within the material—it's not like paint

Clothing the world in swirls of colors to "dye" for, I'm a total trendsetter. I give verve and va-va-voom to all types of materials, from acrylic threads in neon socks to bright paper, as well as imparting a sober dash to shoe leather!

Dyeing goes a lot deeper than just bathing something in colored liquid. My chemical compounds are actually attracted to the substrate material and sometimes need something called a mordant to set the dye. Whereas Precipitate's insoluble colors just sit on top of the material, most of us become bonded to the fiber. I have thousands of different types. Your jeans are stained in indigo—a vat dye, which needs a large keg of nasty alkaline liquor. The world's best-selling dye is Sulfur Black 1, which dyes—you guessed it—your black socks!

W. H. Perkin made the first synthetic dye, mauve, in 1856.

● Earliest recorded use: China, 2600 B.C.E.
● Most expensive: lapis lazuli
● Vegetable dyes: beet, saffron

Dyes

CHAPTER 6
Bright Sparks

This next group of chemical heartbreakers are the life and soul of chemistry. Everything you ever associated with this strange science—weird concoctions, fizzing explosions, and seven types of chemical chaos—you'll find in this energetic bunch. It's enough to make you cackle like a mad scientist! The patron saint of all chemists—Chemical Reaction—provides most labcoat wearers with a job; discovering its secrets and ways to make it work for the good of humankind is a lifetime's study. Now, sit back and let things go with a BANG!

Chemical
Reaction

Reactivity
Series

Combustion

Activation
Energy

Firework

Catalyst

Enzymes

Chemical Reaction

Bright Sparks

✳ A feisty fellow who mixes things up to produce visible changes
✳ Rates of reaction depend on concentration, pressure, and temp.
✳ A chemist's main tool, its workings are essential to industry

I'm gunning to get a reaction. I'm what chemistry is all about. When compounds bump into each other, chemical bonds get broken and atoms, ions, and molecules make new alliances. You can tell if I'm around—compounds change color, thermometers go bonkers, and precipitates appear out of nowhere . . . In short, my process is a chemical change where one substance is transformed into another.

I combine ingredients like a master baker. Sometimes there is no going back to the substances you started with—like baking a cake. I either suck up energy in endothermic reactions or give out energy in exothermic reactions. Chemists who know their reactions can zip around from one product to another, to synthesize the one they need.

The human body has 400 billion chemical reactions per second!

● Speed called: rate of reaction
● Ingredients called: reactants
● Results called: products

Chemical Reaction

Reactivity Series
Bright Sparks

☀ This safecracker tells you how violently a metal will react
☀ Key in reactions of metals with acids and displacement reactions
☀ Tells you how best to extract the metallic bounty from ore

I'm an explosive idea and the secret behind some of the most spectacular reactions! I have a chart that tells you who will win in a head-to-head chemical competition.

I am a blueprint for the reactions of metal. The more reactive the metal, the more readily it will lose electrons to form positive ions. Metals high up on my series are also stronger reducing agents, combining with oxygen to tarnish their shiny surfaces. Wanna know the secret? The number one reactive metal is potassium (steer clear), then sodium (you've been warned), lithium, calcium, magnesium, aluminum, zinc, iron, tin, lead, copper, silver, gold, and, finally, easygoing platinum. Now, wanna see something that will blow your lid? Check out a video of a 5,430 °F (3,000 °C) thermite reaction.

Thermite: iron oxide + aluminum → molten iron + aluminum oxide.

● Fastest reactant: potassium
● Most reactive: potassium
● Least reactive: platinum

Reactivity Series

Combustion
Bright Sparks

☀ This sparky fellow is an unholy burning terror
☀ Fuel and oxidant react to release heat and light
☀ A redox (or reduction–oxidation) reaction

Come closer. I'll warm you up, buddy. BOOM! I'll also leave you with a blackened face. I'm a law unto myself—I can be your friend on a cold night or an explosive nuisance.

I am a highly specialized type of chemical reaction that occurs when a fuel combines completely with the oxygen component of air. This is most definitely an exothermic reaction, which is just a complicated word for "gives off heat." I have energy to burn. As well as my more obvious dangers, my burning generates oxidized products, which are often pretty nasty. For example, fossil fuels burn to produce toxic carbon monoxide, lots of carbon dioxide, plus the acid-rain maker, sulfur dioxide. And when my oxidation reaction is incomplete, I leave minute particles of black carbon soot to waft skyward on my flame.

Materials with low ignition points are prone to spontaneous combustion.

● Combustion = chemical name for burning
● Point substance burns: ignition point
● Incomplete combustion: yellow flame

Combustion

Activation Energy

Bright Sparks

☀ A bright spark who kick-starts Chemical Reaction
☀ The higher the AE, the more energy needed to start a reaction

Every chemical reaction needs some *oomph* to get it going. I am that minimum energy required. If you've ever seen a novice trying to light a fire, angry and covered in soot, you'll know that, unlike $H_2 + O_2$, coal needs more than a spark to combust. But it's not only Combustion who needs my kick. Before many compounds will react, stable chemical bonds must be broken.

Activation Energy

Rusting is a slow reaction, but with low AE since it occurs at room temperature.

● Sources of AE: heat, light
● AE needed to start reaction: energy barrier
● Reaction with low AE: spontaneous

Firework

Bright Sparks

- ☀ A showman with a joyful, impressive exothermic nature
- ☀ This dangerous dude's prime component is gunpowder
- ☀ Invented in China to scare away evil spirits

Firework

Exothermic or what! I'm a colorful showoff pyrotechnician with an explosive personality. I'm a punch packed into a paper tube—an extremely fast chemical reaction. My aim is to live fast and burn bright. Groups 1, 2, and transition metals are mixed with gunpowder (a fiery blend of potassium nitrate, charcoal, and sulfur) to give me my explosion of peacocklike colors.

- ● First known use: C.E. 1100s
- ● Largest manufacturer: China
- ● Largest display: 66,326 fireworks

Barium compounds burn green; magnesium compounds burn white.

Catalyst
Bright Sparks

* Makes reactions go faster but doesn't affect their yield
* Decreases a reaction's activation energy
* This cool cat is not destroyed or changed during a reaction

Chemical engineers love me 'cause I smooth the way for reactions, allowing them to proceed more easily. Despite all the hot stuff going on, I keep my cool and don't get used up in the course of the chemical craziness.

I help produce most industrially important chemicals—you name it, I catalyze it! My "cat-alog" of jobs includes refining petroleum, breaking down chains of Hydrocarbons (called catalytic cracking), and producing ammonia in the Haber process. I often allow intermediate compounds to form, providing a new pathway for a reaction to follow with a lower activation energy. Since less energy is used to start a reaction, it can happen at lower temperatures and faster, too. I can also work by providing a larger surface area upon which a reaction can take place.

CFCs (chlorofluorocarbons) catalyze the breakdown of ozone.

● Top catalysts: zeolites, graphite, platinum
● Most common catalyst: H^+ (proton)
● Unit of catalytic activity: kat

Catalyst

Enzymes

Bright Sparks

- ☀ Catalysts for the chemical processes in living things
- ☀ They make bodily reactions go a million times faster
- ☀ These swampy creatures are almost always proteins

We're enzymes and we live in slime! We drip from your saliva, swim in your soupy stomach juices, and slop around in your cells. Our job is to move along chemical reactions that break down your food, copy your DNA, transmit signals from your nerves and brain, and govern your emotions. We're no ordinary catalysts, though, since we're extremely picky about which individual reactions we assist. Which kind of us a cell stocks determines its metabolic function.

Our protein-gobbling powers also make us powerful commercial chemicals. You will find us breaking down fatty stains in biological laundry detergent, tenderizing meat, and cleaning contact lenses. Our most accurate types are the restriction enzymes at the business end of copying and reproducing your DNA.

Drugs and poisons mess with the normal functioning of enzymes.

- ● Most common on Earth: RuBisCO
- ● Number in the body: about 4,000
- ● Names of enzymes end in "-ase"

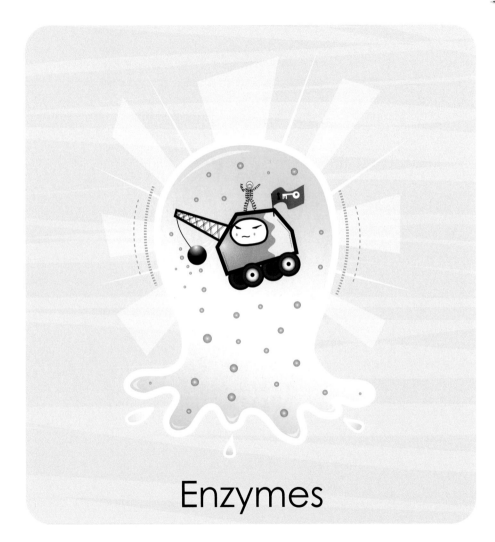

Enzymes

CHAPTER 7
Earthy Resources

Our planet is bursting with chemical surprises, but this resourceful team will keep you grounded. The air, sea, and earth ultimately provide the raw material for all our planet's chemical shenanigans. From the word go, these old-timers have satisfied dabblers' curiosity with materials and substances. They are often found combined in stable compounds, and it can be difficult to separate them. By studying the gang's structure and properties, and ways to purify them, chemists have been able to synthesize a staggering array of new materials and compounds.

Air

Seawater

Rock

Metal

Alloy

Fossil Fuels

Air

Earthy Resources

* An airhead who surrounds the planet
* This wet blanket can hold a great deal of water vapor
* At 60 mi. from Earth's crust, the Kármán line marks its upper limit

Airy-fairy? Think again. I have you surrounded on all sides, and you don't stand a chance of surviving without me, buster! I'm a collection of gases held loosely in place by Earth's gravity. My thin layer, called the atmosphere, wraps around the planet like a cozy blanket. Thanks to my mix of Greenhouse Gases, this heat sink evens out extremes of temperature between night and day and, with the help of Ozone, protects living things from the Sun's radiation.

I'm currently dressed mostly in Nitrogen and Oxygen, but until 2.5 billion years ago, I was principally CO_2, along with choking volcanic nasties, such as ammonia and methane. As soon as photosynthesizing organisms evolved, they began consuming CO_2 and filling the atmosphere with lovely Oxygen—it was a breath of fresh air, I can tell you!

The megatons of dust, pollen, and pollutants don't count as air.

* Nitrogen in air: 78.08%
* Oxygen in air: 20.95%
* Carbon dioxide in air: 0.039%

Air

Seawater

Earthy Resources

* A salty seadog who keeps the temperature of Earth steady
* Its salts are washed out of continental rocks by rain and rivers
* It's evaporated to produce sea salt (mainly sodium chloride)

Avast, ye landlubbers! You may call your precious planet Earth, but you know it belongs to me! I cover more than two thirds of the world's surface and hold 97 percent of its water in my oceans. Underestimate me at your peril!

As a swashbuckling rogue, I'm certainly worth my salt. You see, every 2.2 lbs. (1kg) of Seawater has about 1 oz. (35g) of dissolved salts. While a desert rat might survive drinking me, any thirsty sailor found downing me won't be so lucky—fatal concentrations of salt in the blood cause fits, seizures, and a grisly death. My salt content makes me very different from fresh water. Things float more readily in me due to my increased density, which makes it easier to swim in my waters. I also freeze at 28°F (–2°C), not 32° (0°C), which is why I rarely freeze over. "Sea" for yourself!

A mouthful contains millions of bacteria and thousands of plankton.

* Common salt: NaCl (sodium chloride)
* Salinity of Seawater: 3.1% to 3.8%
* Saltiest closed sea: Dead Sea

Seawater

Rock

Earthy Resources

* A solid, dependable character that makes up Earth's crust
* Made of stuck-together mineral grains (chemical compounds)
* Ores are rocks that contain minerals, gemstones, or metals

I'm totally *ore*-some! I'm the stuff that forms like a crusty scab on the surface of Earth. You can thank me for keeping your feet on solid ground. Look closely and you'll see that all types of me are made up of little grains.

When I'm made of interlocking mineral grains, cooled from molten rock, I'm called igneous; with more rounded grains, I'm called sedimentary. Metamorphic rocks occur when pressure and heat in Earth's crust have altered my minerals. Rocks on the surface are slowly eroded by Water, wind, and weather. Igneous rocks tend to be harder and less porous, but even they get ground down eventually. Rivers and glaciers transport grains of minerals from old rocks to make new sedimentary rocks. It's a cycle that truly "rocks."

Metals and fossil fuels are found buried in rocks, like buried treasure.

● Aluminum ore: bauxite (Al_2O_3)
● Copper ore: chalcopyrite ($CuFeS_2$)
● Mercury ore: cinnabar (HgS)

Rock

Metal

Earthy Resources

* This cooperative fella is found in rock ore—and sure is useful
* Metallic bonds account for its bendability and conductivity
* Most metals corrode in the air by combining with oxygen

I'm your easily persuaded, pliable friend and a great conductor of heat and electricity. Base metals are my reactive bunch who corrode easily and are found tightly bound to their ores. Ferrous metals are mainly magnetic, while noble metals are unreactive. The transition metals bring color to Dyes, Precipitate, and Firework, and many are catalysts that can't be matched.

Metal

An oxidized layer on the surface of metals prevents their sticking together.

● Base metals: copper, lead, zinc, tin
● Ferrous metals: cast iron, pig iron, steel
● Noble metals: gold, silver, platinum

Alloy
Earthy Resources

* Man-made metals who put a little "steel" into Metal softies
* Often made by melting two metals to form a solid solution
* Alloys have a melting range instead of a melting point

Alloy

The Man of Steel, I give a backbone to spineless metals. I make them fit for purpose with properties that better suit their uses. Without me, "supermetal" would be, well, just plain old Metal. I add carbon to iron to make super-strong steel; copper to tin to make super-smooth bronze; copper to zinc to make shiny brass; and nickel to tin to make shape-memory nitinol.

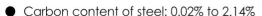

* Carbon content of steel: 0.02% to 2.14%
* Uses for steel: skyscrapers, bridges
* Uses for copper: bearings, statues

Muscle wire is a super-duper, shape-memory alloy.

Fossil Fuels

Earthy Resources

* A powerhouse trio who began life in ancient tropical swamps
* Full of energy, they are extracted by mining, oil wells, and gas rigs
* Carbon compounds buried in the absence of oxygen

As untapped deposits of potential energy, we lie in the dark, secret depths of Earth as vast stores of carbon. When our three types of deposits (oil, coal, and natural gas) react with oxygen in a combustion reaction, you get energy. If the name conjures up images of crumbly old crones, think again. We're formed from the mixed-up remnants of plants and animals that died millions of years ago.

Oil is squeezed out of these deposits or from the fossilized beds of shellfish. It is often found above coal in the earth. Thick crude oil is made of many hydrocarbons, which are separated out by fractional distillation into light, volatile fuels, and gloopy, less-flammable polymers. Natural gas is a much livelier customer and the cream of the crop. My trio provides heat and electrical energy for the entire world.

Fueled the Industrial Revolution of the 1800s and changed the world.

● Age: up to 650 million years
● Coal mined each year: 4.4 billion tons
● Burning releases CO_2 and sulfur dioxide

Fossil Fuels

CHAPTER 8
Chemicals for Life

Life is you, animals, plants—all living things. Life, like all things, uses chemicals and chemical compounds. Many of these are very adaptable, able to turn their hand to the hundreds of functions and chemical reactions that keep life going. Among them, the same elements crop up again and again, in particular carbon, hydrogen, oxygen, and nitrogen. Some, such as oxygen, have mostly been created by life for life. The most amazing is DNA, the miracle molecule capable of replicating itself and building new copies of animals and plants.

Water

Oxygen

Carbon Dioxide

Ozone

Greenhouse Gases

Chlorophyll

Protein

DNA

Carbon

Nitrogen

Water

■ Chemicals for Life

✳ Liquid mover and shaker who covers most of Earth's surface
✳ This wet and wild character is essential for life
✳ A universal solvent that can dissolve many other chemicals

I am the most famous chemical on Earth—everyone knows my formula, H_2O. Although I'm tasteless, colorless, odorless, and neutral in terms of pH, I'm not a sit-on-the-fence type of character. I run in rivers, shaping the land, and collect in the oceans. I hang out as water vapor in rain clouds. I sit frozen solid as polar icecaps.

Most biological processes depend on me. If I'm not present in the correct amounts in your body's cells, the chemical reactions won't go off correctly. Because it takes a lot of energy to make me change state, I soak up temperature changes, protecting the planet from extremes of heat and cold. I transmit light—my transparent nature allows plants to be submerged and because of this food supply, animals can liveunderwater, too.

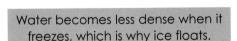

Water becomes less dense when it freezes, which is why ice floats.

● Earth's surface covered by water: 71%
● Volume of water on Earth: 340 million cu. mi.
● The human body is 55% to 78% water

Water

Oxygen
Chemicals for Life

* This nonmetal is the component of air we breathe to survive
* The second most abundant element on Earth
* Its covalent bond splits to form oxides with other substances

Hey! I'm out to get a reaction. There's hardly an element on the periodic table that I won't react with! I'd pick a fight in solitary confinement! I'm the most common element on Earth, included in most compounds on air, sea, and land. But it's as my colorless, odorless gas that I'm best known, because without me, you'd die!

I'm great at dissolving. I slip out of the air in your lungs into your bloodstream and then get transported to every cell in your body, where I power the burning of carbohydrates (sugars and starches) and fats for energy. I also dissolve in Water, which is how fish and other watery animals survive. Cold water can hold more of me than warm, which is why the planet's polar waters have more abundant sealife. I am made industrially by the fractional distillation of liquefied air.

Plants release oxygen into the air during photosynthesis.

● Chemical formula: O_2
● Percentage of O_2 in air: 21%
● Discovered by Joseph Priestley (1774)

Oxygen

Carbon Dioxide

■ Chemicals for Life

* ✳ This fizzy fellow is a major part of the carbon cycle
* ✳ Photosynthesis removes CO_2 from the air and releases O_2
* ✳ CO_2 is released naturally by volcanoes and geysers

I'm a bubbly character, brimming over with good cheer. You find me as the colorless, odorless gas used in sodas to give them a bit of fizz. I am like the meat and cheese for plantlife, who extract me from air during photosynthesis. While plants are gulping down huge amounts of me, the animal world is breathing me out.

But be careful—I can go straight to your head. One percent by volume of me in the air causes drowsiness—you've probably felt this in a hot, stuffy room. Since my freezing point is relatively high, I can be stored solid as dry ice, which allows me to perform a smoky show in stageshows. I'm also used to fight electrical fires. The oceans suck me up, but in the atmosphere I'm a greenhouse gas, causing Earth to get hot under the collar.

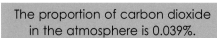

The proportion of carbon dioxide in the atmosphere is 0.039%.

* ● Chemical formula: CO_2
* ● Freezing point: −108 °F (−78 °C)
* ● Goes straight from a solid to a gas (sublimes)

Carbon Dioxide

Ozone

■ Chemicals for Life

✳ A light blue gas; dark blue when liquid; violet-black when solid
✳ Pollutes at low levels and shields Earth at high altitudes
✳ An allotrope of oxygen but less stable—better steer clear!

I'm a two-faced chemical. In polluted areas, I form an irritating, throat-tickling smog. But I come into my own in the upper atmosphere. A thin layer of me, 6 to 30 mi. (10 to 50km) up, is enough to protect Earth from the worst of the Sun's ultraviolet rays. The trouble is, man-made chlorofluorocarbon molecules (CFCs) bust a hole in this layer over the South Pole every year.

Ozone

The largest ozone hole ever was 11.4 million sq. mi. (29.5 km²), Sept. 2006.

● Chemical formula: O_3
● Melting point: −314.5 °F (−192.5 °C)
● Boiling point: −169.4 °F (−111.9 °C)

Greenhouse Gases
Chemicals for Life

- ✹ Bad-boy GGs who horse around in Earth's atmosphere
- ✹ They absorb and reflect infrared radiation back to Earth
- ✹ Have been on the rise since the start of the Industrial Revolution

Greenhouse Gases

Thanks to our ability to absorb radiation, we keep Earth toasty and life moving on. Problems start with heat soaked up by the surface and radiated back. Instead of letting it shoot off into space, we absorb it and beam it back to Earth, which gets hotter. Our numbers are boosted by human activities, such as burning fossil fuels and chopping down forests.

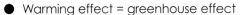

- ● Warming effect = greenhouse effect
- ● Effect due to water vapor: 36% to 70%
- ● Effect due to CO_2: 9% to 26%

Main GGs are water vapor, CO_2, methane, nitrous oxide, and ozone.

Chlorophyll
Chemicals for Life

✸ This miracle molecule has mastered the trick of photosynthesis
✸ Puts the green in greenery and allows plants to feed and grow
✸ Grabs sunlight to power these chemical shenanigans

I am the green goddess, the soul of the natural world. In plant leaves, you find me in blobs (or organelles) called chloroplasts—tiny factories producing the food that plants need in order to grow and develop. The key is a chemical reaction called photosynthesis: Water is taken up through the roots and carbon dioxide from the air, before they are converted into oxygen and sugar-food (glucose, a kind of carbohydrate) in the presence of light.

My ability to absorb light is what makes the reaction run so smoothly. You see me as green because I absorb the blue and red frequencies of the visible light spectrum and reflect the green—leaves turn yellow when I break down in the fall. Plants are a food source for most living things. So it's only fair to say that I feed the world!

Photosynthesis: water + carbon dioxide + light → oxygen + glucose

● Chlorophyll "a" formula: $C_{55}H_{72}MgN_4O_5$
● Size of chloroplast: 0.0004 in. x 0.00012 in.
● Used as a food coloring (such as in pasta)

Chlorophyll

# Protein

■ Chemicals for Life

- ✹ This complex character gets its oar in everywhere
- ✹ A coded genius involved in most things in your body's cells
- ✹ Forms complex organic molecules, folded in different ways

I make your body tick, marshaling chemical reactions in your cells, speeding up reactions (as enzymes), and allowing DNA to replicate. My long polymer molecules are made of combinations (sequences) of 20 types of amino acids, which fold differently according to their sequence. The instructions for making me are right there in your genes.

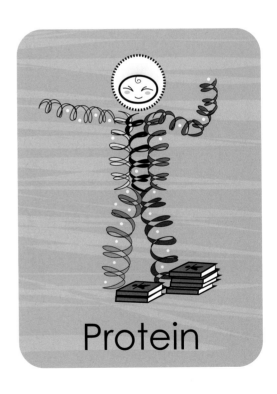

Protein

Swedish chemist Jöns Jakob Berzelius named proteins in 1838.

- ● First described by Gerardus Mulder
- ● First Protein sequenced: insulin
- ● First insulin sequencing: F. Sanger (1955)

DNA

Chemicals for Life ■

※ An amazing molecule, the twisted original that can copy itself
※ "DNA" is short for "deoxyribonucleic acid"
※ Every single living organism contains DNA

DNA

Since the dawn of life, my coded information has allowed the living world to be built, maintained, and reproduced. My pair of molecular backbones twist around each other in a double-helix shape. When unzipped and read by molecules called ribosomes—with the help of enzymes—I enable the proteins in your body's cells and their chemical innards to be built.

● DNA first isolated: 1869
● Double helix discovered: 1953
● Discoverers: J. Watson, F. Crick, R. Franklin

DNA molecules in your body are repaired every eight seconds.

Carbon

Chemicals for Life

- The fourth-most-abundant element in the universe
- The basis of life, it's stored in plant and animal tissue
- Organic chemistry studies compounds containing carbon

I'm a shapeshifter who can morph into many forms. You can't pin me down! I can be clear, crystalline, superhard, nonconducting diamond, or slippery, electricity-conducting, grease-monkey graphite, or atomic chicken-wire graphene, or smarty-pants buckyballs.

The key to my nonmetal marvelousness is my amazing, multifunctional bond-forming, which allows me to connect to others of my kind in long hydrocarbon polymer chains. In this form, I make up all organic matter. On top of that, as inorganic CO_2, I'm absorbed by plants, which use me for food, and dissolved in the oceans, where I'm put to use in the bodies of sea creatures. Eventually, I cycle back into the air when I am exhaled by animals or absorbed into the earth when dead organic matter rots.

> More often than not, I'm unceremoniously dumped in poo.

- Carbon in oceans: 36,000 gigatonnes
- World's strongest material: graphene
- Biggest exporter of graphite: China

Carbon

Nitrogen
■ Chemicals for Life

✳ This usually unreactive type has a highly explosive sting in its tail
✳ An amazing fertilizer but can pollute and poison water courses
✳ Nitrogen-compound ammonia produced in the Haber process

I'm a steady Eddie. Although I make up more than three-fourths of air, I keep to myself, hanging around in tightly bonded, twinned pairs of atoms. Although you won't normally see me making a fuss about things, I don't suffer fools gladly. My triple covalent bond is so strong that those who break it often create explosions.

I'm vital to a mind-boggling array of compounds—you'll find me in chlorophyll, DNA, and protein. Since plants cannot consume me directly as a gas, most of them have to find me in the soil—and they're hungry for me! This is why, as ammonium or nitrate compounds, I'm spread on fields as a fertilizer. I also lurk in the bottoms of beer cans, in clever little things called widgets, put there because my tiny bubbles give beer a lot of foam.

Antoine Lavoisier called nitrogen "azote," meaning without life.

● Chemical formula: N_2
● Percentage of N_2 in air: 78%
● Discovered by: Daniel Rutherford (1772)

Nitrogen

INDEX

GLOSSARY

Alkali A chemical base that dissolves in water.

Amorphous A solid without order to its internal structure.

Base metals The most highly reactive metals in the reactivity series.

Bond The links between atoms formed by the interaction of their outer electrons. There are three types of bonds: ionic, covalent, and metallic.

Burette An instrument used during titrations to determine concentration. It is a vertical glass tube with a volumetric scale and a tap on the bottom.

Caustic A substance that burns skin.

Centrifuge A machine that uses rapid rotation to separate substances of different shapes or densities.

Concentration The number of particles of a chemical in a certain volume.

Covalent bond A chemical bond in which two or more atoms share electrons.

Crystal structure A solid with an ordered internal structure.

Diffusion The process by which particles spread through a solid, liquid, or gas. In gases and liquids, diffusion is helped by Brownian motion.

Dissolve When a solid mixes completely with a liquid, forming a solution.

Electron A negatively charged subatomic particle, found orbiting the nucleus of an atom.

Electron shell Electrons slot into certain fixed energy levels around an atom, called shells. Only electrons in the outer shells interact with other atoms or ions.

Endothermic Describes a chemical reaction that absorbs heat energy.

Exothermic Describes a chemical reaction that gives out heat energy.

Internal energy The movement of atoms or molecules in a substance. Internal energy can be increased by heat or excitation with electromagnetic waves (e.g. microwaves).

Ionic bond A chemical bond between ions, held together by the electrostatic attraction between positive and negative ions.

Neutron A subatomic particle with no charge, found in the nucleus of an atom. It's the heaviest part of an atom.

Noble metals The most unreactive metals in the reactivity series.

Nucleus The center of an atom, containing protons and, in all elements except hydrogen, neutrons.

Oxidation A type of chemical reaction in which a substance loses electrons.

Oxide A compound containing oxygen, formed in an oxidation reaction. Metal oxides are often rusts or tarnishes on the surface of metals.

Photosynthesis A chemical reaction that takes place in plants: sunlight and carbon dioxide are converted into sugar and oxygen.

GLOSSARY

Polar A covalent molecule with an uneven arrangement of its electrons, giving it a slight electrical charge at its ends.

Proton A positively charged subatomic particle, found in the nucleus of an atom. The number of protons an atom has is also its atomic number.

Radioisotope An unstable isotope, which is radioactive.

Reduction A type of chemical reaction in which a substance gains electrons.

Salt Compounds formed when acids are neutralized. These ionic compounds can dissolve to release positively and negatively charged ions.

Solution A liquid mixture of two or more substances.

Solvent A liquid that dissolves another substance.

State of matter The state in which a substance is found at a particular temperature and pressure. There are three broad states of matter: solid, liquid, and gas.

Surface tension A force between the molecules in a liquid that pulls them together—it allows bugs to walk on water without breaking the surface!

Synthesis A series of chemical reactions that result in a predetermined product. This process is used to produce chemicals industrially.

Vacuum A space empty of matter, found inside thermometers and in outer space.

Volatile Describes a substance that reacts chemically with other substances.